There was a soft distillation of sound as a loud crack pushed bluntly through the cottony air. A wisp of powdered bone sighed and hung like an apparition lost faintly in the summoning of early morning daylight. Fluid pitter pattered quietly upon the concrete as bruised brain matter rolled lazily from the back of the skull and my hand rested, heavy under the weight of smooth white shell. The wet glimmer of silence found the dance between my lips and the draping skirt of my eyelids. Both quenched into stillness by a flood of immediacy. The slow throb of the womb of wordless grace echoing off the broken storefront windows across the street. Reflecting a pastel slurry of jagged clouds. Somewhere within them, a small storm murmured on…

WATER MeDIA

Also by Lucky:

These Things I Crave
Violent Words for Beautiful People
O.G. Indigo
Inside Dark Light

Contact: sakulryder@gmail.com

Portrait by Jamie-Leigh Gonzales

Water Media
©2007 Lucky Ryder

ISBN 978-1-7774688-4-2

All rights reserved.

No part of this publication may be reproduced, distributed or transmitted in any form or by any means, electronic, mechanical, photocopying, recording or otherwise, without the prior written permission of the author.

WATER MeDIA

Lucky Ryder

STATICONTENTS

13	A MORE VISCOUS KIND OF ME
14	SHAFTS OF EARTH FORM THE TREES WE HANG FROM
16	MY LENGTHENED HOURS
18	BED OF BROKEN WINDOWS
20	HEAVY HEARTS, WET FLAMES, WE'VE FINALLY FOUND A HOME
22	THE HEART IS A PUMP
25	STILL
26	DORMANT SKULLS BEGIN TO SWELL
27	WHITE RABBIT
28	LIVE FROM THE STAGE
29	HEADPHONES
30	IRIS WIND TUNNELS
33	TO RIDE SKIMMINGTON
34	SHAW
35	SUBSTANCE REMAINS
37	IF THIS PHONOGRAPH WERE A FLOWER
38	BLISTERS
40	FLAGS
41	A FLOODING INCESSANTLY
42	MASTODON (I WISH I WAS)
45	THE THINGS WE CLAIM IN FRONT OF PHOTOGRAPHS
47	EXCUSES, EXCUSES
48	I BELIEVE IN INVERTEBRATES

49	SALINE
51	AWAKE ON A TRAIN
53	START AS YOU MEAN TO GO ON
54	WHILE I'M STILL HERE
55	WHAT IT MEANS TO BE APART
56	FIRST NARROWS
57	NO MAN'S LAND
58	PRETENDING TO DIE
59	STONED APE
61	FINGER PRINTS
63	IRIS
64	ANGELS IN ABSENTIA
66	PAPER AND PENCIL
67	TINY GHOSTS
68	I'M 9 TODAY
70	ACOUSTIC SMOG
71	CAMPFIRES ON CONIFEROUS
72	SPHERES AND DOORS

*Sitting on phone book
listening to cracked glass records.*

*Drinking out of vinyl tea cups
in frayed cuff sweaters.*

*Powdered noses
smoking cigarettes
basking in the soft crone.*

*Off the hook muted moans
coming from the next room.*

We don't have to go home...

A MORE VISCOUS KIND OF ME

Just past the snow blinds
my hands, rest
deep in my pockets.

Hot coils twine around my fingers
sewing spirals
through the knuckle
and bone stitching comatose.

(You can't see me) remember?

The shutters are powder blue
keeping the audio tightly fermented.
I drink the clicks and cuts
through paper thin teeth.
Bending the moisture inward
like flakes tattoo my enamel.

I am deep in the bank
with an upturned nose.
Thick wool cuffs
frame these wrists
and a severed sense of time.

My feet, are all that is left.

SHAFTS OF EARTH FORM THE TREES WE HANG FROM

Motorize these wooden gears
to cinch my wrists closed.
Moss slowly replacing
the slag in my pockets.
On my dead body
life is grown.

Of all the earth rising
in steady shafts and quills
it was these ones to turn to trees
and string me high from boneless limbs.

These things I crave
from day to day,
and still my feet
won't touch the ground.
I am not the knave
that I have crowned.
But on the record,
staved limbs straight,
I am hanging where I belong.

My rotting pockets
fold like birth canals
pierced upon sharpened hips.

Rupture at the feeding
of these receding fontanels.
Thickening, growing,
until this living shell
consumes me fully.

Until it is all that is left.
All that exists.
A refuge for my own disease.
Two square meters
of vital sarcophagi in the trees.

MY LENGTHENED HOURS

You proved the stories true
when you had caught a wisp
of an embalming star's dying dust.

Carved a scarf for the craters
from the Saturn ringlet rocks
spilling over the edges of your eyes.

Anchored in the dirt
and when you're swinging
orbit slowly and wise,
for those stumble that
run fast before the ground.

It is only an exterior,
a crust for the fluid inside.

There would be a widow before me
if I were to spend myself from either.
Within or without.

Claim what the palpitations meant to me
without care for the tremoring day dreams
as they had come to you
would mean there is nothing left at all.

Stringing satellites together
so that I might spend the stone.

I would throb and angulate,
agitate and be nothing of an excuse
but dwindling cold fire.
Still waking sleep abscond bright smoke,
blowing through my hollow frame.

Dangling from sleeves of star dust.
What was left?
You'd be not much more.

Blind

and path covered.

Broken ankle

and stair case heavy.

This brawling love that I birth
is not without apology.

BED OF BROKEN WINDOWS

I could have been the back of an eye,
but I lacked the nerves to know where to look
and I guess that's why I'm patch ridden and septic.
While blows to my windows and a hard left hook
sent me sprawled, ratcheted across
the floor like with swan throat anguish.

Embarrassing blemished seeress
steaming hence this poor sight execution notice.
Birthing glass of water,
crystalline shatter at the siren's call.
I am dazed and I am strapped,
blindsided,
chloroform doused
imbedded against a pock marked firing wall.

These finger slits,
grasp towards my appendages
as hooks carve treasured moons.
Gaping crescent holes that form my heart
to lead to you these precious wounds.

Pulsing magnetic blood clots
draw in the slews of glass
and spat,
severing my sclera.

I've imploded from the frame
with a manual dexterity,
cupping like pincers
and overexposed retina.
Photocells regulate the conservation of parity.

I am feeding on the glass.
My mouth full, if you ask.
Shackles of reflections render clarity.

HEAVY HEARTS, WET FLAMES, WE'VE FINALLY FOUND A HOME

I am fluid.

But not conscious of the ways I show
for I lost my map in the free fall also.
Torn and strewn through the valley
of entwined destroying angel caps.
I have found lodging for myself
under the canopy of these pileus traps.

Where the dark and shadow
conceive of brooding growth.
Sprouting spider limbs
and a gaping yawn
to stretch the river full.
To widely siphon you of your synapse
and finally swallow you whole.

Before we become no one
we sew ourselves into the shadows
and winding through the folds
we come to find a home.

We've room to tongue our swollen lamellae.

I will cradle your ribs late into the gloaming.

The psilocybin rests heavy in our mouths.

Our quills are hollow
and receive the poison
like fiery geysers
and glancing laughs,
straught with purple glass.
Wet flames pressing heavily
against our hearts.

THE HEART IS A PUMP
Sometime su su, sum someti...

Sometimes I stutter.
And I feel foolish.

And when I stutter
and feel foolish
I feel like a child.
Like I do not deserve
to be called growed up.

Those hands, are tto big,
to be yours, you might say.
That hair on your face
and your body
do not belong to you.

Sometimes when I stutter, I beg
to god to let my arms and legs melt,
squeeze & mold into my body
like soft wet dirt.
The kind that drowns worms.

So that i take take up as little space
as p o s   s   i b   l e.

I would roll into the dark place between
the radiator and wall, behind the book case
and I would sing.

Not words though.
No words.

Words are rough
and scratchy.
Obtrusive and brackish
cutting from behind my lips.

But sounds.
Soft sounds I sing into
the back of the book case.
Letting Nicole and Chuck
and William interpret me
through their thick text and iNk.

The sun peels through the blinds.
Dries me of my moisture.
My lips chap, and dry, and cling together
so I no longer sing my sounds.
I, I Hum.
I hum the sounds the clothes dryer makes.
My own humming I would make friends with,
when my parents were taking turns
throwing the phone at each other

and I would roll into the dark space
betweeen the dryer and the wall,
pressing my cheek against the thick dust.
Pretneding the hum and the whoosh
are still as loud as they were
when I ate what she ate
and drank what she drank
and all was blind and right in the world.
When I did not crave the hum and the whoosh
and I did not hum and I did not
sing sounds neither.
I did not wish for melting limbs,
and words were just her heart
certain and steady
beating softly in the distance.

STILL

I've seen you bled of your color before.
Still, I never thought your skin could turn so gray.

I've seen you sick and bed-ridden before.
Still, I never thought you'd be so addicted to the pain.

Wherever did you go on the day you ran away?
Whatever did you think you'd gain?
Still running away, the same.

DORMANT SKULLS BEGIN TO SWELL

Convulsive truant soaked with water and wine.
Spontaneously staggered with teeth. Covering your
scalp with mold from the car crash you hallucinate
about choking ghosts that seethed, striking out from
the newsprint like words caught burning in flight.

I grasped the shaking stalks
that I've sewn between your ribs.

Perched along the mantle curses sent shocks
hollering upon the urn's own ash exploding.

You never clashed with, never noticed,
the raw meat reeking stagnant in me.

Feel deep inside my vase
until you clutch limb and lung.
Stow away inside when the vessel falls
and you'll be the first to accept no fault at all.

And when you breathe the acid
dripping from my stomach's walls,
reach for your own wrists.

This dormant child will begin to stir
and surely die as it exists.

WHITE RABBIT

Today I saw a man in the rain.
Prostrate and helpless on the side of the road.
His face covered in blood. Weeping.

Sometimes do you ever
feel like you have found
everything terrible inside yourself
personified in one horrific moment?

LIVE FROM THE STAGE

I am a shaking jaw and the curvature of shadow.

The tongue against the roof of my mouth.
The dust between my teeth.

(The light turning tears to stars.)

I am so many things

and nothing you can see.

I am a heavy drone of feedback.

Drum tight that I can't speak.
The spotlight dries out my skin,

no wonder I can't breathe.

HEADPHONES

An arched pathway through glass grass
blows softly with the f-train's resonance.

Somewhere
a boy paints his hands blue,
leaving deep rivers in the concrete walls.

Drawn in oak and marked with thick ice
in the fibers of the bark "every day I love"
has been carved with a bass driven hand,
cascading across the page.

Circle waves amplify the rain obscuring
the paint flowing from my headphones.

Somewhere
there is an arched pathway I will find.
Always.
All ways with love.

Softly bending with the splash of cymbals.

IRIS WIND TUNNELS

Shy at dawn, you stood swiftly on chimney tops.

With yellowing phosphorescence under your
eyelashes I mistook you for a blinking owl
caught sharp against the lighthouse.

In alleyways I awaited your low flight.

Careening in cobblestone
you grew from feathers in the wall.
Elongated and slipping razors
through cracks in the brick.
Guiltily gliding along
glinting hints of harvest moon,
hex my shadows.

I accepted greedily.
Drawing the lot into my palms
with a seminal dexterity.
They're tucked away tightly
in the folds of my cheeks.

Against the raining smokestacks
you beat your wings for safety.

Shifting the rift brought these shallows in sight

and though this portal is warm to the touch,
this up drafting wind has all but left me.

These plucked strings only
grow louder with the silence.
Hence my deaf barren water worn excuses
amidst the thousand fiddles you play.

The echoes of such bring a haunt and a blaze.

With cloaks in tattered rags
this loose wind rips a hole in me
known only as cacophony.
Set jettisoned among the novas the day
I first gazed into your compound eye.
I knew from that moment,
that I would never walk again.
Never though would I predict
the tax to be had at the hollowing of my bones.

I can sense the speed that I gain
by the width of the holes in my eyes,
and the desperation of time
by the length of your silhouette
in the distance.

I am lighter than air
with a face drawn from night.

In alleyways,
I await your low flight.

Until the birds fall from the sky
and your monstrosity is strongest among us.

When I will fly fearless through clear skies
to the heart and throat of your resistance.
With soft belly turned upwards,
you will scream a million violins
in collapse against their maker.

My hands are porcupined with slivers,
and my resilience is astonishing.

TO RIDE SKIMMINGTON

Shouts in a vacuum.
Dissipating circa hail storm rates
neither control nor ridicule,
my guest in the doorway.

Tungsten autonomy.
Reflux geometry
reconcile via my visitor input anomaly.
Taunt the discus, but not really.

Holster said distaff
and shouldered accompaniment
by a nuanced procession of jeering neighbors.

Insomniac cavalcade mimics juxtaposition of apnea.

Intermission compliments the hoist duration.

Lost in reception distorted by
bright light and dark visuals
injected in a vak ume.
Not the one you thought you knew.
Please wipe your feet before entrance.
Cleanliness
is directly proportionate to dissonance.

SHAW

Shaw was her name, and a haughty laughter was her color for the cuttlefish on fork rouged like forty grit sandpaper. Betwixt esophagus and larynx dawning a heavy horizontal glow rising in time with wide spread thighs. Her thick lips heave and shift with such happiness that can only be known
by such a woman in her home.

Only such a palate could give way to such a moan. Teasing the teeming seas and wrought with a commotion she alone could bestow.

An acrimonious stare streams from under water eyes and a gloaming slowly rises up from beneath the tide.

Rebellious laughter can fill lone kitchens for only so much time. Before the rivers bare down on bed knobs. Before the rains, before the floods, before a single thrash brings nowhere to hide.

Through the window
I see Shaw empty her refrigerator,
and climb inside.
This is now her only vessel.
Her only home.
The shore fades away while she dines alone.

SUBSTANCE REMAINS

Am I still the reverb?
Is the reverb still here,
cloning the silent excess
in doses along a long line of dimmers?

Am I still
after the vibrato has long since silenced?
Am I a sequin still stuttering after the lights
have long since sustained the post glow fade
towards spiraling shapelessness?

A weight sought and found.
This shaking breath does subdue
a brief lapse of my fluttering jaw.
Buoyant in the dark shades
overlapping dark shades ripple
in the wake of my stillness.

Am I alone after this
long lone line
of stuttering silence?

Exhale.
Inhale.

Does this subdue the darkness?

Does it clone the post glow fade
towards some white light excess?

Exhale.
Inhale.

I am still the reverb
dissipating above this very room,
and long after I am silent
you will know me by
the vibrato of your
waxing fingers waning.

I am still here,
I know you can feel me.

IF THIS PHONOGRAPH WERE A FLOWER

If this phonograph were a flower,
its pollen would disperse across the ears
of all the people I have ever been.
Under a banner of petals,
they would sing into being
the hands I see before me.

BLISTERS

In the reflecting rain we remain lost between the drops.
Drawing long and singular. Simple needle point renders
perpendicular slag soft images in which curve a stiletto
fish eye curb wise, broken heel hedonistic Polaroids.

In your cross-cut demeanor those eyes of yours
slice my photograph in half, but not across
the cobblestone alleyways in which you appear
pastel smudged along your lines.
Like with lingering linguistics
shot straight home from
the shackled stars of the skies.
Skimming reckless and clairvoyant,
cloaked these trench coat throb thighs.

Hungry for just half an hour.
Just twenty-five minutes
of dove down, down time.

When you are dry it has been twelve solid minutes.

We smoke the bodies of those we watched tonight
and with every exploding super nova wine glass laugh,
the last shards spiral outwards to accept our orbit.
Suspecting me of nothing more than playing tempest,
to your oscillation of candle light and heavy drapes.

When you are dry, it has been twelve, solid, minutes.

Breathing heavy, and wet
like an excellent bottle of Gray Monk zinfandel.
So full the room slants towards ceiling fans and lamps
so as to sample as much as is allowed by the gods
before we cork presence,
and regain the mysticism of absence all over again.

Just the way it remains,
night after night, day after day.
This inflection of white light pin prick rain
at the apex of that street there,
I can surely make out the essence
of some sort of door way.

Solid against my palm, still calm.
I can neither breach it's mane
nor close it to the way you say,
swaying closets subjugate my stay.

In this defiance I remain a quivering atom,
a Rodleen scream because
in here I am dry and I am bones,
and you? You remain on hold,
blue in the face, with a dead leaf tone.

FLAGS

Honey,
there are so many shapes
your shadow takes,
when it traipses
out in front of me.

Why,
I could spill like an altar,
spark like a blaze.

Why honey,
you're a shadow
just as fluid as flags.

Why,
I could spill over
like with mud from my heart.
When you pass over my rivers,
I am cleansed by the dark.

When you are not
a thousand fluttering flags.

You are a myriad of shades to my eyes.

A FLOODING INCESSANTLY

Tell me where you went
when I was sleeping on the riverbed.
The clay has cured in the sun.
Our finger prints now so evident.

The wind sings them to us
like a needle upon the record.

A broom in the corner of a potter's hovel.

MASTODON (I WISH I WAS)

3:30am.
I am drawn to semi consciousness by the fluctuating of
some dim halogen, emitting from a faraway machine on
the distant side of the room. I imagine it is just the
refrigerator at home as a weighty click,
from silence into heavy buzz fills the white halls
like a thousand flies through a garden hose.

It's surprising with tubes pouring like fingers
from my arms how much I seem to know,
when I'm so lost inside that hose.

The morphine is strong, and spins me from flesh
and bone towards information in binary, tracing cave
paintings across my lines of syntax like 1's and 0's
turning off, and on.

Again, my attention catches the flocking buzz, sharp
and cutting the hot fluid air. A galleon of blazoned
knives and steel feathers peculate my auricle in a
staccato sestina into the depths of my temporal cortex.
Sustaining a constant static in my subconscious.

I dream of bone yards and elephant graves.
Twenty-dollar bills, mirrors and blonde braids.

Spaced out between the white lines
I dream in a harsh film grain,
littered with cigarette burns.

Our soft heads, smashed in,
folded over the steering wheel
after a wrong turn at the lights that night.

In my dreams it becomes clear
though I hear you in the distance,
you are gone now.

And nowhere near here.

The sirens and ambulance doors are birdcalls
and epitaphs standing three meters tall.

At time of stretcher conception, I am ten thousand
kilograms of leathery hide and slit eye tear geysers
stretched across ten thousand kilometers of 'why?'

Even for me with shattered ribs
and a punctured lung I don't need to tell
you that that is stretched, too goddamn thin.
Too goddamn thin for children like me.
For children like us.

We are not of twenty-dollar bills.

Mirrors. Blonde braids.
Sunken cheekbones.
Mirrors and bloody noses.

Throat shaped steering wheels.
Airbags that never deployed.

We were children
with dusty palms
and stale airways.
We were not as invincible
as we once thought we were.
We were not the elephants
we believed ourselves to be.

We are as extinct as the mammoth.

A Mastodon,
I wish I was.

THE THINGS WE CLAIM
IN FRONT OF PHOTOGRAPHS

After a few hours the fish around my ankles grew
in curiosity as to the roots of my body. So suddenly
invading their salt water inlet and as that curiosity
took the best of them, began churning and clasping
around hypothermic feet like weathered paper clips
scraping against cardboard.

In my thinking about how little time there is
I come to the realization that that, is all I have.

The silent sound of crickets drowning.
Faux pretense of dangerous creatures
juxtaposed in a rigid tableau.

For the past twenty days I have been playing vagrant
to the wine bottles scuttling across the deck. Cowboy
to the clocks on the wall with a mouth full of numbers,
pockets full of paper, and a tongue of battery acid I
stood at the right hand of Jacques Cartier.
The balls of our bare calloused feet
thick in the sternum of the St. Lawrence.
We watched as waterfall fortresses rose up from fields
thick with corn and at that moment, we knew for
certain that we would never truly learn for ourselves
what it meant to discover.

To evade our certainty, homes nearest the estuary
were the first to go. For every arrow they drew
I lay still in the inlet, battered by waterfalls
carp tangle in my hair until nightfall,
when the stars ran red.

The silent sound of crickets drowning.
An upheaval with means to no end.
The crackling of torches against thatching,
the dousing of landscapes in ash.

There are these losses that I cannot explain away.
The way my wrists drop in a sudden fit of paresthesia.
A white-knuckle motif I cannot believe
where through the course of leaves,
we retreat, we leave.

Like the way the wind is outside,
torrential yet still, still in me.
But I had taken a fistful since I touched shore,
and that, that was good enough for me.

To know I never knew.
To cradle emotions I'll never feel,
bathe in waterfalls I've never seen,
to eat of a land, I've never touched.
To know I never knew.
That was good enough, good enough for me.

EXCUSES, EXCUSES

You have changed so much.

You are nothing like
the latest engine's first breath
on my riveting skin.

Pockmarks.

Are the streets that you sleep on?

Soft cells.

I'll be your scanner of binary
in the heat of the night.
If you let me.

And I'll be your scanner
if only you could turn me on

the right way.

What way?

I can't say.

I BELIEVE IN INVERTEBRATES

Then it fell apart from the mouth first.
Wide fender lips the spoke tooth hub jaw.

The day the root canal ran dry.
The angler fish drowning in wind,
slapping against the shale floor
stirs the sex up in me.

Then it fell apart in an unusual form of falling.
A collapsing inward safe from downward.
The same way bird's wings fold when
thrashed against the ocean's surface.

The earth's core, throat wide open.
Puckering volcano invert,
boiling to raise the feathery scales.
Pimpled and tingling.

The gulls drowning in salt.
The fish flounder in wind.
Shriveling like slugs entombed mud holes
crack and cut my hands to brittle starfish ribbons.

As the sex simmered, I became a lark between asphalt
and tire treads, driven to tear the damn thing apart.

I cannot help the feeling of biting my lip.

The days I grasp the pulsing vein
crushed the sternum under lock and love,
again, and again, and again.

Calm shivers in mud holes.
Scales and feathers.
Tread marks on my chest
I heave and concave.
Wax and I wane
with unfortunate ambiguity,
and a luxurious distress.

SALINE

If there is any electricity left,
I should hope to burn what is left of you.

If there is any electricity
after the power lines become my broken arms
and I tear far away to the oceans with teeth,
sharp as airplanes.
Conductive thoughts
like steel wool brains,
pouring skin like wood stains
and finger nails, thick as asbestos
like the goddamn mouth of your shame.

Of what you took from me.

And if there is any electricity
left at all inside of me
then I should hope
to burn you all away.

I should hope to burn
all sight of you away.

AWAKE ON A TRAIN

I will wipe the stripes
of your suit from you
and across the valleys,
curving with the whisp
of clouds atop still trees.

You lean with the winds when
you swing your hips just so
to bend your crooked knees.
With the pulling of the tracks
you squeeze by,
                  by,
                          by.
You squeeze by, you and I.

The rain soaking our sides to the bone.
I can taste your well stoked coals.
Freshly oiled gears.
Moving parts that are sung
perpetually into the dawn.
The dim sun nesting into
our deep curves.
Our horizon.
The landscape will be
our setting daughter,
our rising son.

Alone and unseen.
Dancing heavy to the
churning engine sounds.

Are we asleep while moving?
I am not awake
and yet still breathing
on you, the conductor.
Swaying deep and slow as you go.
Stoke the fires when the sun dips low.
The rows of lamps flicker and flow.
When the stripes you sew
spread into the valleys
you will be my haunting, heavy glow.

Breathe on small engine
and let your hanging breath show.

Breathe on small engine.
Breathe on.

START AS YOU MEAN TO GO ON

Heavy bridges in the heat
of an open field of clouds.

Rising on the bass.
Coasting on the treble.

Start as you mean to go on.

Guiding as the ambience
glides to sing that song.

Lips in an 'O' shape.
Tongues that will have their way.

We are one of these today.

My feet are clean
in the air condensing.

My wings soak the light from heavy.

We'll start as we mean to go on
and find as we have been found.

WHILE I'M STILL HERE

Listen to Aphex Twin's I Care Because You Do.
Drink chai tea with milk.
Laugh all the time and cry just as often.
Dance to sounds that aren't music.
Let the wine run down your chin.
Think of those you don't speak to.
If you steal don't get caught.
Your crooked glasses
aren't as noticeable as you think.

Sing.
Play the piano however you know how.
Never stop creating.
Smoke cigarettes like there's always half a pack.
Don't hide from your own happiness.
Never say no to a possible new relationship.
Stay up to watch the sun rise.
Love the weather no matter what it is,
it's proof that the earth is still alive.

WHAT IT MEANS TO BE APART

I play an old voicemail from you
that I have listened to
more times than I can count.

Today,
I come to it in search of solace,
to find only the reassurance
that you are so, so far away.

And I am left knowing,
knowing what it means to be apart.

FIRST NARROWS

Six months from now I watch us up there
from deep inside this heavy mellow earth.
Cradled underneath frosty mornings.
Resting easy atop summer nights.
Smoking cigarettes at the edge of the dock
with our toes submerged in the sea.
Your eyes straight as stars ahead of you.
Mine straight as branches ahead of me.

I watch you in my peripheral.
Humming a tune in time with the waves.

I have no idea what you are thinking.

I feel your fingertips trace ellipses
up and down my spine,
hip to hip and back again.

We each have means to our own ends.
We are the angels that guide us to them.
To one another we are backed by spirits.
We will speak again in whispers and secrets.
Hold our breathes and know, that we are with us.

NO MAN'S LAND

Bordered by walls,
heavy bolt cutters and leather gloves,
an opponent for the razor wire.

Atop of the rough stone I see you in the distance
silhouetted by the brick and spray paint skies.

Though you've always been a black construction
paper cut out on the horizon, I've always loved
the conversation that careens between us.

I'm certain that if I was patient enough
I could catch a glimpse of the electricity
arching between our palms.
Ascending/receding.

Segregation is a powerful conductor.

Our minds. Our hearts.
Our arms are lightning rods
recording individually.
Produced in no man's land.
Compilations while we are sleeping.
Tracks played in tune with the clouds.

This is will make for an excellent start.

PRETENDING TO DIE

There's these skull and bones
of paper cranes
that I keep inside my thermos.
Ribs and eye sockets
soak deep and coffee logged
every time I hit the road.

It's getting to be a lot like silt on a river bed.

Fossils I drink the oil of seem
to clear me of my congestion.
But I'm afraid of a lack of fossil fuels.
So lately those skull and bones go unappreciated.

The world
is a confusing place.
I can no longer keep track
of the things I take
with a shaker of salt,
guilt and grace.

STONED APE

Bits and pieces of information
form suddenly shifting vertical villages.
Temples of syntax stoking collective longevity.

The tribes are a blur.
Water color in tall dry grass.

We know each other as quick teeth
and ascending feet. Hands on the ladders.

Tempo is instigated as crescendo is assembled.

Volume.

Shreds of notation fall in cadence
along similarly tunneling floors.
Bridges are built in the space of a breath.

I remember you only as memories I cannot recall.
The fibers in blank canvas
reach outwards towards creation.

Silence and organization are the foundation.

The mind is a cube.

Something has to change.

FINGER PRINTS

Don't you know
that these are the last skies
to underlie your atmosphere.

I have closed spaces,
with artificial oxygen.

Superfluous air flows through the filters
and filling our minds once again,
we breathe.

The wavering in our breath
is constant and haunting.
Comforting.

In this room I could pull you in.
We could layer the moments together.
In this room our shoulders grace the walls.
Your fingertips and the heels of your hands
rest high up against my chest.

I could pull you in, tighter.
Tighter than you are with lungs.

I'll be your inhaling exhalation
under these last, and latest skies.

I could hold you close.
I could hold you, near.

Away from the rust and rain,
the porous atmosphere.

The turnstiles
and neon lights
for nothing nights.
Where no one is.
Where no one goes.
They are gone now,
and nowhere
near
here.

Well, I could hold you close
don't you know.
I could show you
how to breathe.
Don't you know, don't you see.

I could tell that our apocalypse was brooding.

I just prayed that you'd believe.

IRIS

...And there you were twelve years later.

Behind blistering grey eyes.

I watched your silhouette
pillar through the center of my palms
to take off across the grass.

Lengthening in the distance.

I bled from the inside
as your shadow rose in an apex
of fashioned quills and
wrought iron fountains ablaze.

Am I as beautiful as I used to be?
When your teeth were lost so deep inside of me?

ANGELS IN ABSENTIA

Where there's an umbrella
I will obtain the means.
The blood around my fingernail
seems shaped the same to me.

I was given a fistful
from the bark load.
Taking it not for granted
I constructed myself a tree.
Now I sit high above the dirt,
the quarry and granite.
Safe from the rains
with a somewhere to be.

A somewhere to be free and silent.
To pick my scabs and watch them bleed.
Bang my head upon the branches
until I dream new born dreams.

Discover the chaos in me
is the math of nature.
The movement of nurture
merely a massing of sutures
that confuses and bugs the senses.

While in the end I am left

with nothing but fences,
short cut grasses, houses
built never with questions
but somehow with answers.

Now tell me my dear,
where have we gone?
Where have we been?
What is any of this
supposed to mean?

What of the water?
What of the media?
What of everything
we thought we knew?
Washed away.
Photographs we've never seen.
Angels in absentia.

PAPER AND PENCIL

...caught my instability in a sudden wave
of communication. That pressing jaw caught
my wave in a sudden rising platform of stability.
Those white tongue dark noises
shunted the wind from my coven of live wires.

Tall drinks of water litter the living room.

I unbutton my blouse
in the soda shoppe bathroom.
I am not wearing a bra
and it feels liberating to be so exposed.
You tongue at my nipples and I brew.
The automatic dryer is dreaming my dreams
and it is so comfortable
to be so controlled right now.
Right here my movements are so sudden.
A disease, I am happy to share.

One day we will smoke pencil shavings
and speak of math.

I want to be the one to kill language.
One day, I want to be the one to kill.

TINY GHOSTS

Mum. Pause. Escalate. Oxygen.
Is a rarity that I will never pine for again?
My lungs are weighed down
with better things now.
Provisions. Lipstick.

On a regular basis as a child, I was caught
in the hotel basement inhaling Ziploc bags.

No one understood
I just needed a proper coating.
A better lining for all of us. This
will be something I needed all along.

You'll see.
My lungs will burst but the bags just stretch.

I'm happy again. I love you,
Mum. Pause. Escalate.
Oxygen. You bred.
Oxygen. I fed.
Escalate. I did. Escalate. I'm dead.

And at a hotel I could never see from down here.
(I know you will see that this was for the best.)

I'M 9 TODAY

Today I learned some new things.

That I can feel like how I imagine
an open field of tall grass feels.
When the warm air moves
in a whooshing breeze shape.
The sky is so black and blue.
Black and blue, but clear also.
The space above my head is so empty
I can hear harpsichord music in the wind.

Today I learned what it means
to be so cold on the outside,
and so gosh darn warm on the inside.
Like a pineapple or other good fruit.

Or maybe like Earth.

Yea, a lot like Earth.
Molten hotness inside.
While rocky and tree covered
with lots of perfect green moss all over the outside.

Today I learned how I can feel like
I'm all covered with moss, but not really be so.

That's only how I feel,
and I think I understand now.

Because I am a person and in 9 more years
I'll be a much older person, and older people
get to make older people decisions.
Like feeling however they want to feel.
But it's sad, because I don't think
they all remember that they can do that.

But it is also very happy.
Because I'm 9 today,
and today I learned
that I can feel however
I feel like feeling.

I'm molten hotness on the inside,
and perfect green moss on the outside.

ACOUSTIC SMOG

Watch the trees curl like snowballs
as the dragons roll by.

Breathing in the steam
that fills the hot springs
we wade in, waist deep.

Invited as guests to a feast
in the home of the harvest leeches.

Blood let conscription
from our toes to our thighs.

Ten thousand doorways scatter our legs.
This is beginning to feel a lot like television.

CAMPFIRES ON CONIFEROUS

I think it's time
that you came with me.

I have twenty dollars
for our next head phase.
So, let's find comfort.
Let's find peace
under the sun
and purple dawn.

We are doing well.
We are almost there.

SPHERES AND DOORS

High upon the turtle's back.
Softly swaying, with each printing step.
Nomadic in my own right.
I will spend the rest of my life
searching, for a home.

www.ingramcontent.com/pod-product-compliance
Lightning Source LLC
Chambersburg PA
CBHW072136070526
44585CB00016B/1700